Beans, broken cups and pebbles...
Gather them up and let's make some marvelous

MOSAICS

This edition published in 2013
By SpiceBox™
12171 Horseshoe Way
Richmond, BC
Canada V7A 4V4

First published in 2013
Copyright © SpiceBox™ 2013

ISBN 10: 1-77132-052-4
ISBN 13: 978-1-77132-052-8

CEO and Publisher: Ben Lotfi
Editorial: Ania Jaraczewski
Creative Director: Garett Chan
Art Director: Christine Covert
Design, Layout & Illustration: Charmaine Muzyka
Production: James Badger, Mell D'Clute
Sourcing: Janny Lam, Desmond Hung

For more SpiceBox products and information, visit our website:
www.spicebox.ca

Manufactured in China

3 5 7 9 10 8 6 4 2

CONTENTS

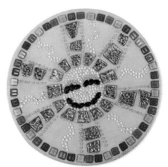

PROJECTS

WHAT IS A MOSAIC?

Have you ever pressed pebbles into a pattern in the sand? Then you've made a mosaic! A mosaic is a picture or pattern made up of pieces of tile, stone, glass, marble, shells or other objects set into cement or plaster. It's a form of art that lets you create designs using anything your imagination can come up with!

We Greeks did more than just carve marble statues of gods and heroes!

HOW IT ALL BEGAN...

People started making mosaics over 4,000 years ago. Some of the first mosaics were made in ancient Greece, using different colored pebbles pressed into clay or mud that would later dry. Wealthy families covered their floors with mosaics in patterns that looked like woven or braided rugs. That way, there were no carpets to clean!

The oldest mosaics were created thousands of
years ago. Can you imagine making a mosaic photo
frame and having someone in the year 4013 use it
to decorate their home? How cool would that be!

This is the sort of pattern that you will find in ancient Greek mosaics that looks a lot like a rope or braid. Try making this with different colored beans to create the same effect.

But one too many wealthy Greeks must have tripped over the pebbles sticking out of their own floors, because eventually someone came up with a way to make mosaics flatter. Artists started using **tesserae**—little tiles made of marble, bone and precious stones.

Enjoy a rainy day outside by pressing pebbles into a muddy patch in your garden to make a mosaic. What other objects can you find outdoors to use in your mosaic art?

Middle Eastern artists made mosaics with geometrical patterns. Try using different colored objects to create your own shapes and designs.

9

Hey, some of our mosaics took thousands or even millions of tiny tiles to make! It wasn't easy!

MOSAIC MADNESS

Not to be outdone by the Greeks, the ancient Romans soon began making their own mosaics. They preferred to use glass tiles called **smalti** to make glittering, colorful images that were as detailed as paintings. The Romans became so skilled at this art that they could create a mosaic on

This mosaic has so many details, and such tiny tesserae, that it looks almost like a painting! If you want to try this effect, use a three-hole punch to punch out lots of different colored bits of craft paper that you can use to create your own detailed mosaic picture.

the ground that showed realistic bits of food littered everywhere, so that no one would notice if something was accidentally dropped from the dinner table. On the other hand, the different methods they tried led to some pretty odd results, like three-legged horses and bent spears... but everyone makes mistakes!

This spectacular ceiling is made with gold-leaf mosaic tiles. Try cutting up bits of aluminum foil or a foil wrapping paper to create a similar effect.

Wow! Can you see how the different shades of color blend together to create a lifelike, 3D effect?

Some mosaics took dozens of workers years to make! Phew!

In the Middle Ages, mosaics were used mostly in churches to show stories from the Bible. Shiny gold-leaf smalti made their way from the floor to the ceiling, covering huge arched vaults. But sometimes the artists forgot that the ceilings were so far above the people who would be looking at them, they made the details of the images so small that no one could actually see them! But there's one thing they did get right: they created some early attempts at 3D effects with their mosaics, making people and animals seem to come right out of the walls.

The Romans were not the only ones ahead of their time. It seems that Islamic artists paid attention in geometry class when they were kids, because they made their mosaic patterns with math skills that were not recognized until hundreds of years later. Islamic countries also used mosaics to show religious scenes, although the artists were careful not to put pictures of human figures on the ground, because they realized that walking all over holy people was probably a bad idea that would lead to all kinds of trouble.

Mosaics were expensive and took a long time to make. Eventually, other forms of art became more common, but we can appreciate the beautiful works left behind by mosaic artists over the centuries.

The Portuguese people explored the world in ships full of black and white stones that they used as ballast. Once they set up a new colony, they would unload their stones and make lovely mosaic-paved sidewalks and roads, and then fill their now empty ships with gold and riches to take back to Portugal!

There are world records for the largest mosaics made with cars, toast, umbrellas and doughnuts!

MOSAICS TODAY

Mosaics continue to be popular today. In Barcelona, Spain, many parts of the city are covered in colorful mosaics that were made by Antoni Gaudí in the early 20th century. Now popular tourist attractions, many of his mosaics are actually made of recycled trash! He took bits of broken bottles and china and turned them into art, which goes to show that you can use any material to make mosaics.

Gaudí used recycled glass, broken plates and even pieces of a china doll in his mosaics. What a great way to turn trash into treasure!

Some of the first video games designed, like "Space Invaders" and "Tetris" have pixels or squares that make them look like mosaics. Can you think of any other games that remind you of mosaics?

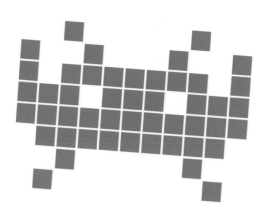

French artist Invader has even made a graffiti version of mosaic art. He uses little tiles to create the pixelated spaceships from the video game *Space Invaders*, and sticks them onto walls in cities around the world. The inspiration for mosaics can come from anywhere!

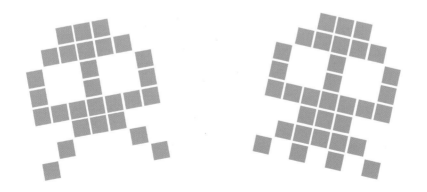

HOW TO USE THE TEMPLATES

Do you want to make beautiful mosaics like the ancient Greeks and Romans did? A good way to get started is by using the foam tiles and templates in this kit. Here's how:

STEP 1

Pick out a template you like from the back of the book, or choose one from inside the kit box.

STEP 2

The template shows you which colors to use where. Each color has a number. Look at the numbers on the template and find the foam tiles in the right color.

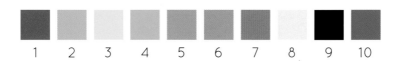

1   2   3   4   5   6   7   8   9   10

HOW-TO USE THE TEMPLATES

STEP 3

Peel the adhesive backing off
each tile and stick the tiles onto
the squares on the template,
using the numbers as a guide.
Keep going until you've covered
all the squares on the template.

Tip:

Artists don't really like paying attention to rules. If you want to use different colors than the templates suggest, then go wild!

Now that you've practiced your mosaic skills, you're ready to tackle the other projects in this book. These projects are all inspired by the art of mosaic, but use all kinds of materials and techniques. Use your imagination to create your own unique artworks as well!

COOL BEANS!

PHOTO FRAME

Food was a popular subject in Roman mosaics. Sometimes the food even fought back— one mosaic shows a huge fish swallowing a fisherman whole! You can even use food instead of mosaic tiles. Rescue beans, popcorn kernels and dry pasta from becoming lunch by turning them into a fun picture frame!

WHAT YOU NEED

- Cardboard (a recycled cereal box will do)
- Marker
- Scissors
- Assorted beans
- Craft glue

STEP 1

Draw a heart, oval or other shape in the middle of the cardboard. Cut out the shape to make a window.

STEP 2

Without using glue at first, arrange the beans on the piece of cardboard in different ways until you get a pattern that you like.

COOL BEANS!

PHOTO FRAME

STEP 3

Once everything is where you want it to be, start gluing the beans in place. It's a good idea to start at the edges and work your way in.

Find a photo of yourself and a friend to put in this funky frame!

SEA GLASS

CANDLE HOLDER

The ancient Romans not only made mosaic tiles and other objects out of glass, they recycled glass too! You don't have to wear a toga to recycle glass in your own home. You can use an empty glass jar or an old water glass to make a cool new candle holder!

WHAT YOU NEED

- Empty glass jar from recycling
- Glass tiles (purchased from a craft shop)
- Glass glue

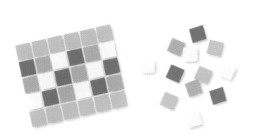

STEP 1

Plan out the pattern you want to use by arranging your pieces on a flat surface. Use glass tiles or pieces of sea glass.

STEP 2

Using glass glue, start gluing the pieces to the jar. Start with the bottom row and work your way up.

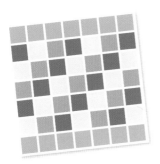

STEP 3

Once you've finished, let the glue dry completely before putting a candle inside. Ask an adult to light it for you, and watch the colored light flicker!

29

LETTER PERFECT

NAME SIGN

Tired of your parents and siblings barging into your room? Things haven't changed much from the times when the ancient Romans made mosaics with pictures of guard dogs, warning people to stay off their turf! You can make a sign with your name and hang it on your door to remind everyone that your room is private property!

STEP 1

Draw the letters of your name on a piece of cardboard and cut them out. Paint the letters black.

LETTER PERFECT

STEP 2

Plan out where you want your mosaic pieces to go before you start to glue them down.

STEP 3

Glue all your pieces in place. To make a sign for your door, glue the letters onto a larger piece of cardboard and hang it up!

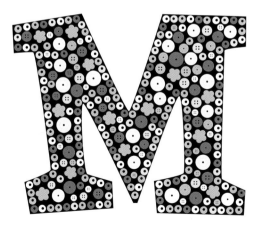

Bling out your door
sign with glittery
sequins and beads!!

SEA STAR

BEACH-THEMED MOSAIC

The very first mosaics, made thousands of years ago, were created using simple objects found outdoors, like stones and seashells. You can use colorful pebbles, sea glass and shells to make a beach-themed mosaic that will make it feel like summer all year long.

WHAT YOU NEED

- Piece of cardboard, or pre-cut wooden shape
- Pebbles, glass marbles, seashells
- Sand (optional)
- Craft glue

STEP 1

Draw a shape on a piece of cardboard and cut it out. If you want, you can glue a thin layer of sand onto the shape.

STEP 2

Plan out where you want your pieces to go before you glue them down.

STEP 3

Glue all the pieces into place and let them dry.

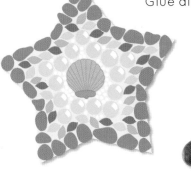

Banish away the winter blahs by bringing the beach inside!

THE WRITE STUFF

JOURNAL COVER

Don't you agree that plain walls and floors are boring? Over the centuries, people have covered ceilings, floors and other surfaces with mosaic art to decorate them and make them beautiful. Why don't you do the same with a notebook or journal that has a plain cover? Use your mosaic-making skills to spice things up!

WHAT YOU NEED

- A journal or notebook with a blank cover
- Pieces of colorful fabric
- Fabric scissors
- Marker
- Tacky or craft glue
- Sequins, beads, buttons

STEP 1

Draw the outline of a picture onto the front of your journal or notebook. Cut up some scraps of colorful fabric into small pieces.

STEP 2

Glue the pieces of fabric to your journal to fill in your design.

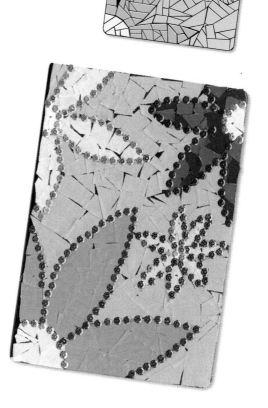

STEP 3

Add some sequins, beads or buttons to make it shine!

WILD TILES

CLAY MOSAIC

Now it's time to go on a treasure hunt through your home and find all kinds of objects to use in your next piece of mosaic art!

WHAT YOU NEED

- Air-drying clay
- Assorted objects such as: dried pastas, beans, rice or lentils, buttons, bits of broken clay pots or china, scraps of fabric and anything else you think would make a nice mosaic.

STEP 1

Using the air-drying clay, create the shape that you want and flatten it out. Make sure that it's at least a 1/2 inch thick.

STEP 2

Start laying out the pieces to make a design. Make sure you press the pieces firmly into the clay so they don't fall out.

STEP 3

Fill in the rest with a cool pattern. Let the clay dry completely before picking it up.

With this project you can use beads, bits of china, pennies, pebbles, seashells, glass tiles, marbles or anything else you come up with!

PIECES OF YOU

PICTURE MOSAIC

The ancient Greeks didn't have cameras, so they often used mosaic art to make portraits of themselves. But why go through all the bother of setting hundreds of tiny little tiles into plaster? You can make a cool mosaic using just a photo of yourself!

STEP 1

Cut your photo into a bunch of small squares.

STEP 2

Starting from one corner, glue the pieces onto the cardboard, row by row.

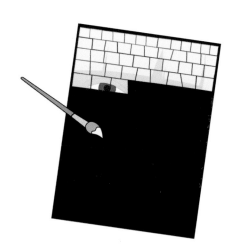

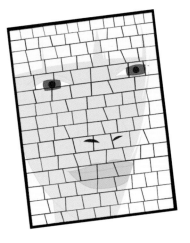

STEP 3

Let your mosaic dry before giving it to someone as a gift!

GREETING CARD TEMPLATES

After you've completed these fun templates (see page 20), try cutting out the shapes and pasting them onto the cards provided in the kit. Surprise someone special with your mosaic creation!

(see page 20)

7	7	7	7											7	7	7	7
7	8	8	7											7	8	8	7
7	8	8	8	7			7	7	7	7			7	8	8	8	7
7	8	7	8	8	7	7	7	8	8	7	7	7	8	8	7	8	7
7	8	7	7	7	7	8	8	8	8	8	7	7	7	7	8	7	
7	8	7		7	8	8	8	8	8	8	7				7	8	7
7	8	7		7	8	8	9	8	8	9	8	8	7		7	8	7
7	8	7		7	8	8	9	8	8	9	8	8	7		7	8	7
7	7		7	8	8	8	8	6	6	8	8	8	8	7		7	7
7			7	8	8	9	8	8	8	8	9	8	8	7			7
			7	8	8	8	9	9	9	9	8	8	8	7			
				7	8	8	8			8	8	8	7				
					7	8	8			8	8	7					
						7	8	8	8	8	7						
						7	7	7	7	7	7						
					7	8	8	8	8	8	8	7					
				7	8	8	8	8	8	8	8	8	7				
			7	8	8	8	8	8	8	8	8	8	8	7			
			7	7	7	7	7	7	7	7	7	7	7	7			

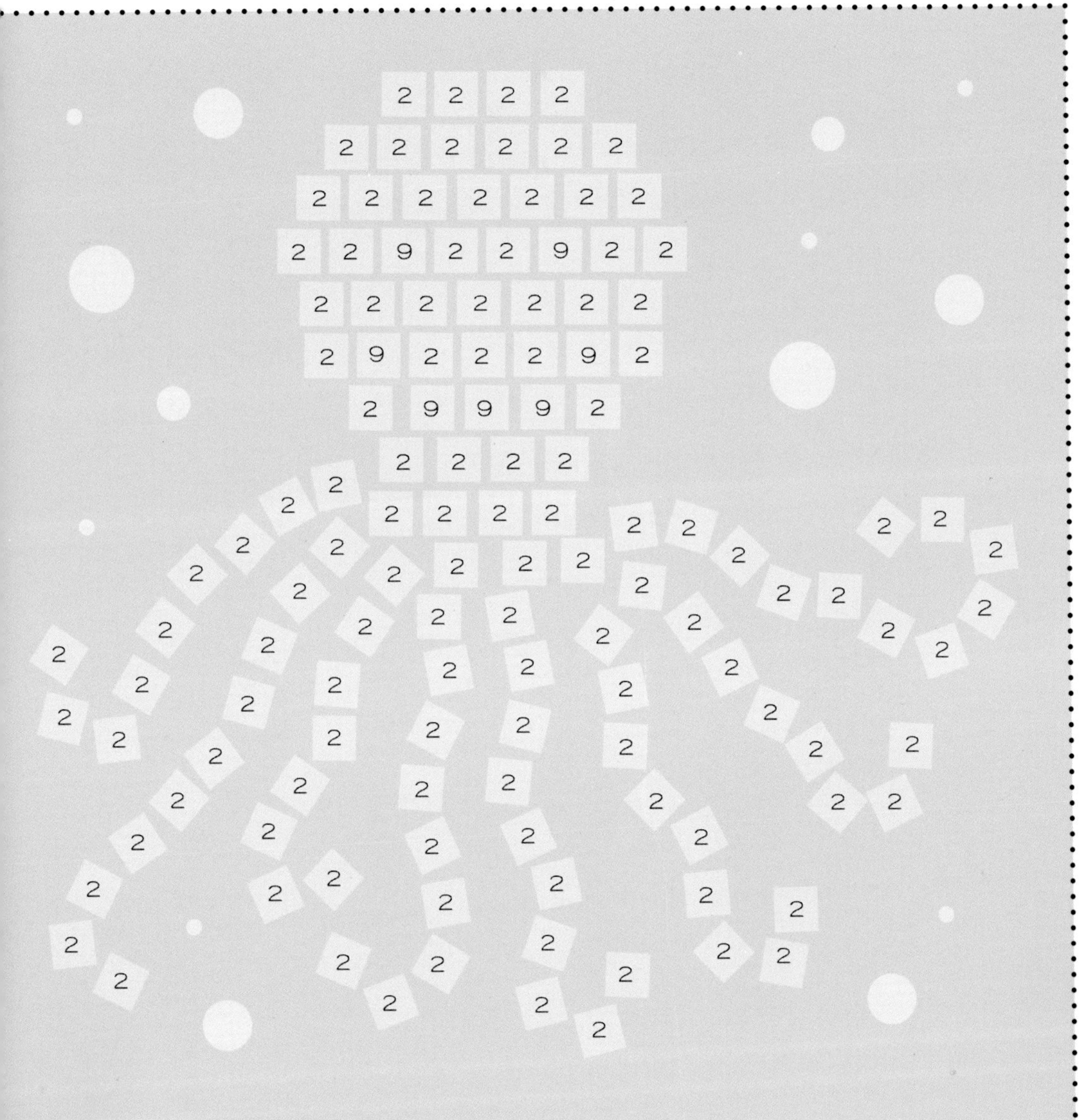

GREETING CARD TEMPLATES

5	5	5	5	5	5	5	5	5	5	5	5	5	5	5	5	5	5
5	5	5	5	5	5	5	5	5	5	5	5	5	5	5	5	5	5
5	5	5	5	5	5	5	5	5	5	5	5	5	5	5	5	5	5
5	4	4	4	4	5	5	5	5	5	5	5	10	5	5	5	5	5
4	4	4	4	4	4	5	5	5	5	5	10	3	10	5	5	5	5
4	4	4	4	4	4	4	5	5	5	10	3	3	3	10	5	5	5
4	4	4	4	4	4	4	4	5	10	3	3	3	3	3	10	5	5
4	4	4	4	4	4	4	4	10	3	3	3	3	3	3	3	10	5
4	4	4	4	4	4	10	3	3	10	10	3	10	10	3	3	10	5
4	4	4	4	4	10	3	3	3	10	10	3	10	10	3	3	3	10
4	4	4	4	4	5	5	3	3	3	3	3	3	3	3	3	5	5
5	4	4	4	4	5	5	3	3	3	3	3	3	3	3	3	5	5
5	5	7	7	5	5	5	3	10	10	3	3	10	10	3	3	5	5
5	5	7	7	5	5	5	3	10	10	3	3	10	10	3	3	5	5
5	5	7	7	5	5	5	3	10	10	3	3	10	10	3	3	5	5
5	5	7	7	5	5	5	3	3	3	3	10	10	3	3	3	5	5
4	4	4	4	4	4	4	4	4	4	4	4	4	4	4	4	4	4
4	4	4	4	4	4	4	4	4	4	4	4	4	4	4	4	4	4
4	4	4	4	4	4	4	4	4	4	4	4	4	4	4	4	4	4

GREETING CARD TEMPLATES

5	5	5	5	5							5	5	5	5	5	5	5
5	5	5	5	5	5					5	5	5	5	5			
5	5	10	5	5	5	5	5	5	5	5	10	5	5				
5	5	10	10	5	5	5	5	5	5	10	10	5	5	5			
5	5	10	10	10	10	10	10	10	10	10	10	5	5	5	5		
5	10	10	10	10	10	10	10	10	10	10	10	10	5	5	5	5	
5	10	10			10	10			10	10	5	5	5	5	5		
5	10	10	9		10	10	9		10	10	5	5	5	5	5		
5	10	10			10	10			10	10	5	5	5	5	5		
5	10	10	10	10	10	10	10	10	10	10	5	5	5	5	5		
5	10	10	10	10	3	3	3	3	10	10	10	10	5	5	4	4	5
5	6	6	10	10	10	3	3	10	10	10	6	6	5	5	4	4	4
5	6	6	6	10	10	10	10	10	10	6	6	6	5	5	4	4	4
5	6	6	6	10	10	10	10	10	10	6	6	6	5	5	4	4	4
5	5	6	6	10	10	6	6	10	10	6	5	5	4	4	4		
5	5	5	10	10	6	6	6	6	10	10	5	5	5	4	4	4	4
5	5	5	5	3	5	5	5	5	3	5	5	5	5	5	4	4	4
7	7	7	7	7	7	7	7	7	7	7	7	7	7	7	7	4	4

```
5 5 5 5 5 5 5 5 5 5 5 5 5 5 5 5 5 5
5 5 5 5 5 5 5 5 5 5 5 5 5 5 5     5
5     5 5 5 5 5 5 2 5 5 5 5 5     5
5     5 5 5 5 5 2 2 5 5 5 5 5 5 5 5
5 5 5 5 5 5 5 2 2 2 5 5   5 5 5 5 5
5 5 5 5 5 1 1 1 1 1 5 5 5 5 5 5 5 5
5   5 5 1 1 1 1 1 1 1 5 5 5 5 5 2 5
5 5 5 1 1 1 1 1 1 1 1 1 5 5 5 2 5 5
5 5 1 1 1 9 1 1 2 1 1 1 1 5 2 2 5 5
5 5 1 1 1 1 1 1 2 2 1 1 1 2 2 2 2 5
5 5 5 1 1 1 1 1 2 1 1 1 1 5 2 2 5 5
5 5 5 5 1 1 1 1 1 1 1 1 5 5 5 2 5 5
5 5 5 5 5 1 1 1 1 1 1 5 5 4 5 5 2 5
5 4 5 5 5 5 5 2 2 5 5 5 5 5 4 5 5 5
5 5 4 5 5 5 5 5 2 5 5 5 5 4 5 5 4 5
5 4 5 5 5 5 5 5 5 5 5 4 5 4 5 5 5 4
5 4 5 5 4 5 5 5 4 5 5 4 5 5 4 5 5 4
5 5 4 5 4 5 5 4 5 5 5 5 4 5 4 5 4 5
```